PERSONAL AIRCRAFT

Thanks to the creative team:
Senior Editor: Alice Peebles
Fact Checking: Tom Jackson
Picture Research: Nic Dean
Design: 38a The Shop

Hungry Tomato®
A division of Lerner Publishing Group, Inc.
241 First Avenue North
Minneapolis, MN 55401 USA

For reading levels and more information, look up this title at
www.lernerbooks.com.

Main body text set in Avenir Next Condensed 12/14.

Library of Congress Cataloging-in-Publication Data

Names: Harris, Tim, 1957– author.
Title: Personal aircraft : from flying cars to backpack helicopters /
    Tim Harris.
Description: Minneapolis : Hungry Tomato, [2018] | Series: Feats
    of flight | Audience: Ages 8–12. | Audience: Grades 4 to 6. |
    Includes bibliographical references and index.
Identifiers: LCCN 2017061419 (print) | LCCN 2017057006
    (ebook) | ISBN 9781541523821 (eb pdf) | ISBN
    9781541500945 (lb : alk. paper)
Subjects: LCSH: Personal propulsion units–Juvenile literature.
    | Private planes–Juvenile literature. | Drone aircraft–Juvenile
    literature.
Classification: LCC TL717.5 (print) | LCC TL717.5 .H37 2018
    (ebook) | DDC 629.1/4–dc23

LC record available at https://lccn.loc.gov/2017061419

Manufactured in the United States of America
1-43763-33623-3/14/2018

PERSONAL
AIRCRAFT

by Tim Harris

HUNGRY
TOMATO®

Minneapolis

CONTENTS

FLYING SOLO

A car that can take off, fly over a flooded road, and land again on the other side sounds like a great science fiction story but not something that could really happen. Well, after years of work by engineers, it is a reality. Flying cars are being built. They are one kind of personal aircraft, and there are other kinds too.

Faster and cleaner

Personal aircraft are faster, more comfortable, quieter, and cleaner than ever before. They can take off without the need for a long runway and can squeeze through narrow spaces. Personal craft are lighter than large planes so they don't use as much fuel. For these reasons, they are used increasingly to carry people and things around—for search and rescue or just for fun. Read on to find out more!

Four forces

All flying craft, small or large, have four forces acting on them. Lift raises them off the ground, while gravity pulls them down. Thrust drives them forward, and drag holds them back. For aircraft to become airborne and move forward, lift has to be greater than gravity and thrust greater than drag.

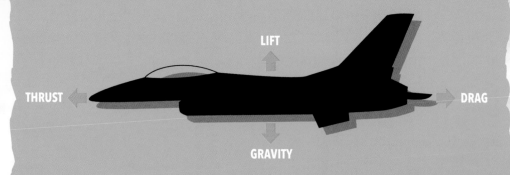

LIFT

THRUST

DRAG

GRAVITY

The DeLorean DR-7 will be one of the first personal electric planes when it takes to the skies, probably in 2018.

MICROJETS

There is a plane that flies as fast as a jetliner but is small enough to fit on the trailer of a car. The Bede BD-5 is the world's smallest jet-powered aircraft, with a wingspan of just 17 feet (5.1 m). Its sleek **fuselage** is made of **fiberglass** over an **aluminium** frame.

▲ Despite its small size, the single-seater Bede BD-5 microjet has a range of 230 miles (370 km) and can hit a maximum speed of 320 mph (515 km/h).

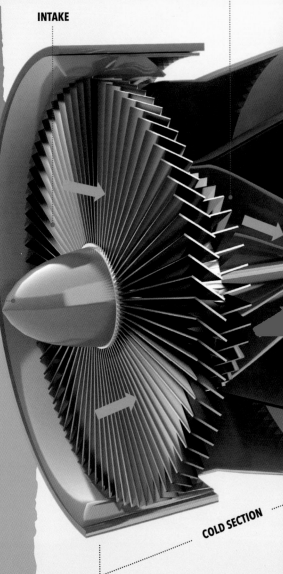

INTAKE

COMPRESSOR

Air inlet

COLD SECTION

How a turbojet engine works

A fan sucks air into the front of the engine. Inside, the blades of a **compressor** spin at high speed, squeezing the air. Fuel is sprayed into the squeezed air and an electric spark lights the mixture. The burning gases expand and blast out through the exhaust at the back of the engine. As the jet of gas shoots backward, the engine and the aircraft are thrust forward. The hot air passes through a second group of blades: the turbine. When the turbine spins, it also turns the compressor and keeps the engine running.

Microjet power

The Microjet 200 is another powerful but tiny plane. Unlike the Bede, it has two turbojet engines, one on either side of the fuselage, which can lift it up to 30,000 feet (9,150 m). It is used for training pilots, and its **cockpit** has room for a flying instructor and a student. The Microjet 200 can cruise at 288 mph (463 km/h) and fly as high as the biggest airliners.

▲ *A Microjet 200 at Farnborough Air Show, England*

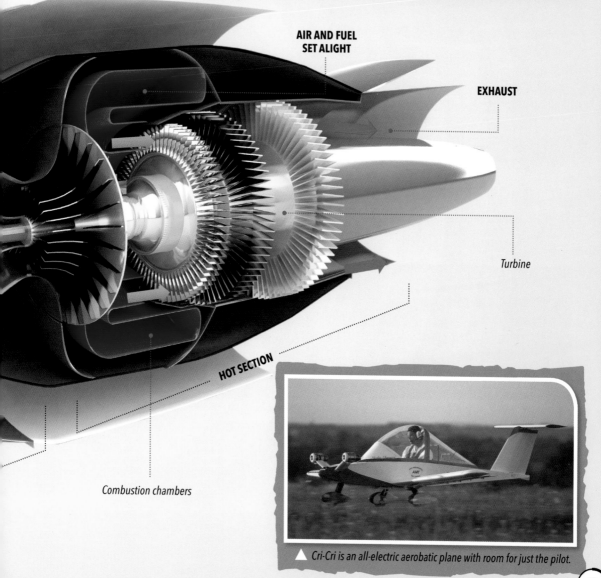

AIR AND FUEL SET ALIGHT

EXHAUST

Turbine

HOT SECTION

Combustion chambers

▲ *Cri-Cri is an all-electric aerobatic plane with room for just the pilot.*

FLYING CARS

The Terrafugia Transition is a car–and a plane! This amazing vehicle drives just like a normal car on a road. But if there is a holdup, such as bad traffic or a broken bridge, it can change into a light aircraft to avoid the problem. In less than a minute, its wings fold out to turn it into a flying machine.

If Transition runs into dangerous flying conditions, its pilot lands it on the nearest road, folds in the wings again, and switches to highway **mode**. With its wings folded in, Transition is small enough to fit onto the trailer of a car so it can be towed back to storage.

Folding wings

To fold the wings away after a flight, the pilot doesn't even need to leave the cockpit but simply pushes a button to activate the folding mechanism. This takes less than a minute.

▲ Terrafugia Transition on the road with its wings folded

Even faster

The engineers who built Transition are now planning an even more remarkable flying car, called the TF-X. Although only slightly bigger than Transition, the new vehicle will have room for four passengers and fly twice as fast. The pilot will be able to direct it with a steering wheel—or hand over control to the onboard computer.

▲ Terrafugia TF-X is larger and faster than Transition.

▲ With its wings extended, Transition can fly at more than 100mph (160 km/h).

SEAPLANES

Many personal aircraft are flown for fun. One such leisure plane is the two-seater Icon A5, which is amphibious—it can take off from water or land.

When it splashes down on water, Icon skims over the surface on two hollow seawings, which keep it afloat. When it lands on solid ground, the pilot lowers a **retractable** undercarriage with wheels, just like on an ordinary plane.

▲ Icon A5 doesn't need an airstrip; this one has just landed on the ocean.

Seawings

The seawings beneath Icon A5 keep the plane stable when it's on water. If one of the seawings is punctured so that water floods in, partitions called bulkheads inside it ensure that only part of the seawing fills up with water. A pump then sucks the water out again.

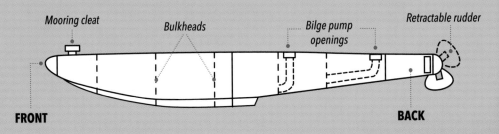

Mooring cleat

Bulkheads

Bilge pump openings

Retractable rudder

FRONT

BACK

Propeller

Behind the cockpit, Icon's powerful engine turns a propeller, which can quickly **accelerate** the craft to 109 mph (176 km/h). It can fly 400 miles (640 km) before it needs to refuel, and after landing, its wings fold up in less than two minutes, so that Icon can be loaded onto a trailer.

Icon is fast and **maneuverable** in the air.

Safety parachute

Many safety checks are run before any aircraft flies, so it is very unusual for anything to go wrong. One clever safety feature of the Icon is a huge parachute that will open if there is a problem with the plane's engine while in the air. The parachute will float the plane slowly and safely to the ocean or ground.

SUPERDRONES

Imagine you need to cross to the other side of town megafast. Wouldn't it be great to have a vehicle that carried you high over roads and buildings to your destination quickly and comfortably? Well, soon there may be one, and you might not even need a pilot's licence!

Scientists are developing the amazing Ehang 184 autonomous aerial vehicle, which is so advanced it doesn't need a pilot. All the passenger needs to do is type in the destination on the craft's touch-screen display. The onboard computer passes this to a command center, and the craft is autopiloted to its destination.

Ehang's onboard battery turns four pairs of propellers to lift the vehicle high above buildings and roads and drive it forward.

Human cargo

Ehang 184 is like a large drone—an unmanned flying vehicle that carries packages, emergency medical supplies, and other cargo. But Ehang is designed to transport humans rather than material cargo. It is very lightweight yet strong, capable of carrying the weight of a large man at 60 mph (100 km/h) for half an hour.

▲ Ehang from above (left), with a pre-programmed flight plan

▶ Ehang's cruising altitude is 1,640 feet (500m).

▲ Since it runs on electricity, Ehang doesn't pollute the air and is also very quiet.

PARAMOTORS

Imagine the thrill of a paramotor flight. With an engine and propeller strapped to your back, you hang beneath a multicolored wing made of strong, lightweight fabric. The whirring propeller drives you away through the air and you slowly gain height.

Paramotors are lightweight sports aircraft that are easy to fly. A simple control starts and stops the engine, and the pilot changes direction by pulling cords attached to the wing. After a day's flying, the paramotor can break down into pieces and packed into a car. These craft do have one disadvantage, though: they are definitely for fair-weather flying and don't perform well in windy conditions.

▲ A foot-launch paramotor consists of a small engine and a propeller strapped to the pilot's back, all **suspended** beneath a fabric wing to provide lift.

▼ Wheel-launch paramotors sometimes have space for two pilots, who sit on a cart, usually with three wheels.

Record-breakers

Paramotors rarely travel at more than 50 mph (80 km/h), but the most skilled pilots can do amazing things with them. In 2007, Ramón Morillas Salmeron flew from mainland Spain over open ocean to the island of Lanzarote, a distance of 700 miles (1,100 km). Two years later, he claimed another record when he flew his paramotor to the incredible height of 25,000 feet (7,600 m).

◀ *A paramotor is suspended on high, beneath a large, colorful wing.*

How a two-stroke engine works

Stage 1

A mixture of gasoline or oil and air is drawn into the crankcase, which is then shut by a valve when the piston is near the top of the **cylinder**. A spark from the sparkplug ignites the mixture.

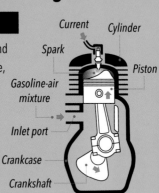

Current
Cylinder
Spark
Piston
Gasoline-air mixture
Inlet port
Crankcase
Crankshaft

Stage 2

When the fuel-air mixture ignites, it expands, pushing the piston down. As exhaust gases leave, a vacuum is created and the piston is drawn back up. This process is repeated rapidly. Each time the piston is pushed, it turns the **crankshaft**, which turns the propeller.

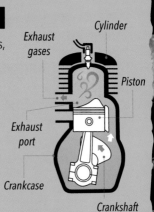

Cylinder
Exhaust gases
Piston
Exhaust port
Crankcase
Crankshaft

ELECTRIC PLANES

Lilium is the world's first vertical takeoff and landing (VTOL) aircraft built for personal use. It combines great speed with an amazing ability to take off and land in a very small area, such as a landing pad on the roof of a building or even a large garden.

Lilium is a battery-powered jet. It can fly faster than most helicopters. Since it is powered by batteries, it is very quiet–if it does take off from someone's backyard, the neighbors won't complain about the noise! Lilium has thirty-six small ducted fans (see opposite), twelve at the back of each wing and six on either side of the cockpit. At takeoff, the pilot points the wing flaps down to produce vertical lift. Once airborne, the pilot tilts the flaps horizontally to produce forward thrust.

FUSELAGE

COCKPIT

Superfast taxis

Two doors lift from the sides of Lilium's cockpit to allow the pilot and a passenger in and out. Its German engineers are now planning a five-seater version that will be suitable for providing a very fast taxi service!

Winged door

▲ *Lilium can fly 190 miles (300 km) before its batteries need recharging.*

Cockpit

Ducted fans

A ducted fan is a small but powerful propeller inside a cylinder. The cylinder encloses the propeller blades, reducing air disturbance (turbulence) at the tips of the blades. This makes the propellers quieter and more efficient.

Ducted fan propeller

Rear wing

Front projection

FAN PROPELLERS

To take off, Lilium's ducted fans are turned down to direct thrust toward the ground.

AUTOGYROS

These lightweight flying machines have long, rotating blades overhead and a propeller at the front or rear. An engine turns the propeller, and this gives the craft the forward thrust it needs. Unlike in a helicopter, the long blades are not powered by an engine. They only begin to turn as the autogyro starts to move forward. The onrushing air turns the long blades, and these lift the craft off the ground.

Pulling or pushing?

An autogyro's propeller may be mounted at the front, so the craft is pulled through the air. This is called a tractor configuration. Or, the propeller may be at the back, "pushing" the machine forward (right). This is called a pusher configuration.

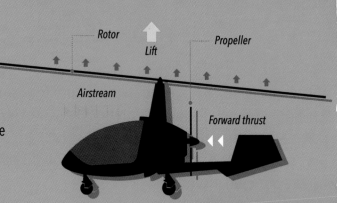

Rotor

Lift

Propeller

Airstream

Forward thrust

The Volocopter

Once completed, the volocopter will be the first manned, fully electric, and safe craft to take off and land vertically. The pilot will use a simple joystick that maneuvers 18 quiet rotors to drive this machine through the air.

Autogyro races

The world record speed for an autogyro is 129 mph (208 km/h). Autogyro competitions are held in Dubai, where pilots race their machines against the clock, flying around a marked course over the desert or ocean to see who can go fastest. They fly two or three circuits around the course and their times are compared.

A Benson B-8MR takes to the sky.

PERSONAL HELICOPTERS

Lots of personal VTOL aircraft take off from the ground as larger helicopters do—with propellers to provide lift. Some are used as search-and-rescue vehicles because they can operate in very difficult and dangerous situations. Others are used just for fun.

The Solo Trek

With one of these personal craft, an experienced pilot can take off from a very enclosed space, then twist and turn in the blink of an eye through narrow gaps between buildings. It can even hover. And if there's a problem with the engine, an emergency parachute lets the pilot down gently.

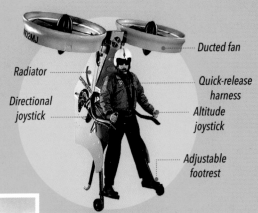

Radiator

Directional joystick

Ducted fan

Quick-release harness

Altitude joystick

Adjustable footrest

▲ Solo Trek's pilot controls the craft from a standing position.

Backpack Helicopter

George Sablier created his own personal helicopter in 1954. A special apparatus prevents the pilot from gyrating with the propeller. Propelled by a six horsepower engine, the device weighed 60 pounds (27 kg) and was said to fly about 31mph (50 km/h).

Film star

The personal helicopter featured in the movie *Agent Cody Banks* was the Solo Trek XFV (XFV stands for "exoskeletal flying vehicle"). It can fly for two hours before it has to refuel and can hover for long periods. If traveling at top speed, it can cover 120 miles (192 km) in this time.

◄ *A Solo Trek about to lift its crew to safety in the movie* Agent Cody Banks.

Airscooter

An airscooter is a kind of personal helicopter. The pilot sits in a cab hanging below two sets of rotor blades. One set turns clockwise, the other set rotates counterclockwise. This setup is called coaxial, and it makes the airscooter easier to control when it is flying. To steer the craft, the pilot simply points the handlebars in the direction he or she wants to go.

WINGSUITS AND WATERJETS

For sheer thrills and entertainment, a jet-powered wingsuit can't be beaten—but it is definitely not for the faint-hearted! Tiny but powerful jet motors are attached to a carbon fiber wing strapped to the pilot's back. Such powered wingsuits can travel very fast, if only for a short time.

Water blaster

If you fancy cruising over the sea, suspended 30 feet (9 m) up on powerful waterjets, the Jetlev Flyer could be the thing for you. An engine floating behind the Jetlev sucks up seawater and pumps it through a hose. Then the water is blasted at high pressure through jets on the pilot's backpack, keeping him or her suspended.

The Jetlev in action

The Jetlev pilot can control the water supply by squeezing a hand-held **throttle**. When the throttle is activated, the high-pressure flow of water starts. Water squirts out of two nozzles behind the driver's shoulders. The force of these jets creates an upward force, pushing the Jetlev up. If the pilot tilts forward, the Jetlev moves forward at up to 35 mph (56 km/h).

▶ Awesome waterjets power the JetLev's driver over the ocean.

Looping the loop

The pioneer of wingsuits is Yves Rossy, who has hit speeds of 195 mph (315 km/h) with his Jetman Jetwing. He once jumped from a helicopter high over the coast of France, fired up the engines of his wingsuit, and crossed the English Channel to England—a distance of 22 miles (35 km)—in just 13 minutes. He celebrated by looping the loop! On another occasion, he and another wingsuit pilot flew in formation with an Airbus jetliner over Dubai.

◀ The Jetman Jetwing is capable of incredible speeds.

▲ Yves Rossy and fellow jetman Vince Reffet flying over the Palm Jumeirah, in Dubai

THE FUTURE

Engineers are working on more comfortable and faster personal aircraft. They are developing new designs for quieter flying vehicles and ones that rely on electricity rather than fossil fuels.

▶ The DeLorean DR-7 will fly with two pairs of wings.

DeLorean DR-7

One of the most exciting of these is the sleek, superfast DeLorean DR-7. This electric VTOL aircraft has two pairs of wings that fold away, reducing the plane's width so much that it can easily be stored in a garage. The DR-7 has room for a pilot and passenger in a fighter-jet **tandem** arrangement. To fly it, the driver can use manual controls—or allow a computer to do all the work. The DR-7's batteries will fly the craft 120 miles (192 km) before they need recharging. It is expected to make its first flight in 2018.

▲ A passenger or co-pilot sits behind the pilot in the cockpit of the DeLorean DR-7.

◄

The Puffin is being developed by NASA (the National Aeronautics and Space Administration).

The Flying Puffin

The Puffin personal VTOL craft will have a very unusual design. It will be very fast, capable of reaching 150 mph (240 km/h), and have a range of 50 miles (80 km). Since it is powered by batteries, it will be very quiet. Unusually, the pilot will lie horizontally when flying the craft.

Backpack helicopters

Designers are also looking at ways of constructing even smaller machines for flight. The backpack helicopter has small but very powerful batteries and **contra-rotating** blades to lift the person into the air. Maybe one day, everyone will have one of these!

◄ *An artist's impression of the backpack helicopter of the future*

HIGHLIGHTS OF FLIGHT

People have always wondered what it would be like to fly. Hundreds of years ago, a man in Spain called Abbas ibn Firnas attached birds' feathers to his arms and jumped from a high tower.

Although Ibn Firnas flapped his wings like a bird, he didn't fly but fell to the ground, hurting his back. This was one of the first attempts to build a personal aircraft. Later, people used kites and balloons to lift them off the ground. Here are some more recent attempts and successes.

1948

After World War II, the US Air Force looked for ways to protect its bombers from enemy attack. One idea was the McDonnell XF-85, a fighter aircraft that was small enough to fit into the bomb bay of a Corsair bomber. Despite numerous efforts, pilots couldn't get the XF-85 to dock with the bomber in flight, so the scheme was abandoned.

1923

The first successful autogyro flight took place in Madrid, Spain, piloted by Alejandro Gómez Spencer. The craft was designed by Juan de la Cierva, who invented the autogyro and built several different versions.

1932

The tiny GeeBee Model R racing plane set a world record for a land-based aircraft–296 mph (476 km/h)–despite having a wingspan of just 26 feet (8 m).

▶ *An artist's impression of Lilium personal jets on a rooftop launch site*

1955

The XRON-1 rotorcycle was a single-seat helicopter designed for the US Navy to use in military maneuvers. This project was abandoned because the vehicles' engines kept overheating.

1973

The Bede BD-5J microjet made its first successful flight. This plane would later feature in a James Bond movie.

2017

The German-engineered Lilium personal jet was the first personal vertical takeoff and landing electric jet.

GLOSSARY

accelerate: to get faster

aluminium: a lightweight metal

cockpit: a compartment for the pilot of an aircraft

compressor: a machine for squeezing something

contra-rotating: spinning in opposite directions

crankshaft: the engine part that turns the up-and-down piston movement into rotational movement

cylinder: in an internal combusion engine, the chamber where the piston operates

fiberglass: a strong, lightweight material

fuselage: the main body of an aircraft

maneuverable: able to change direction suddenly

mode: a way of working

retractable: able to be drawn back in

suspended: held beneath something

tandem: an arrangement with one in front of the other

throttle: a device controlling the flow of power to an engine

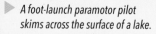 *A foot-launch paramotor pilot skims across the surface of a lake.*

INDEX

The Author

Tim Harris lives in London and loves the natural world, science, and travel. He has written many children's and adults' books for Bloomsbury, Dorling Kindersley, National Geographic, and Grolier. His subjects include the history of engineering, animal anatomy, great battles, meteorology, and geography. Tim has also edited several travel guides, and before entering the world of book publishing, he was deputy editor of *Birdwatch* magazine.

Picture credits (abbreviations: t = top; b = bottom; c = center; l = left; r = right)

1 = Volocopter GMBH. 2, l = Shutterstock. 3, c = Icon Aircraft. 4/5 = Rex Features. 6/7,c = DeloreonAerospace. 8/9, c = NASA. 9, r = Invictus SARL / Alamy Stock Photo. 9, t = ShutterStock. 10, l = Terrafugia drivetofly. 10/11. c = Terrafugia. 11, r = Terrafugia / 12, l = IconAircraft. 12/13, c=IconAircraft / 13, t = IconAircraft. 14, l = EHANG. 14/15, c= EHANG. 15, r = EHANG. 16, l = ShutterStock. 16, l = Alamy Stock Photo. 16/17, c = ShutterStock. 18/19, Lilium GmBH. 20, l = Alamy Stock Photo / 20/21 = GBAgyros. 22, l = Solotrek. 22/23 c = Everett Collection Inc / Alamy Stock Photo. 24, r = GettyImages. 24/25, c = Ali Haider/EPA/Rex/ShutterStock. 24, r = Rex. 26 l = NASA. 26, r = DeloreonAerospace. 26/27, c = DeloreonAerospace / 27, r = NASA. 28/29, c = Terrafugia. 30/31, c = Shutterstock. 32, t = Icon Aircraft.